Behind the Carnival

John Lyons

Smith/Doorstop Books

Published 1994 by
Smith/Doorstop Books
The Poetry Business
The Studio
Byram Arcade
Westgate
Huddersfield HD1 1ND

ISBN 1 869961 54 4

Typeset at The Poetry Business
Printed by Swiftprint, Huddersfield

Cover by the blue door design company

Distributed by Password (Books) Ltd.,
23 New Mount Street, Manchester M4 4DE

The Poetry Business gratefully acknowledges the help of
Kirklees Metropolitan Council, Yorkshire & Humberside
Arts and North West Arts.

Previous publications
The Lure of the Cascadura (Bogle L'Ouverture 1989)
The Sun Rises in the North (with Chatterjee, Martin and
Sissay) (Smith/Doorstop Books 1991)

Acknowledgements
Thanks are due to the editors of the following publica-
tions in which some of these poems have appeared:
*Poetry Review, Oxford Poetry, Pennine Platform, Ambit, Can
You Hear (Oxfam Anthology*, Piper Pan Macmillan
Children's Books).

CONTENTS

To Agnès and members of Off The Page

THE RACONTEUR

(For the Midnight Robber)

From shadows under sandbox tree
I heard spirits' voices
like silvery whisperings:
How in the beginning,
the serpent in Eve's ritual
was a man-snake mapepire.

And after tricks with his tail,
he found a place to hide
among balisier flowers.
His rankness spoiled their fragrance
stiffened their silken orange flames.

Tales were told of owl and black bird
how they challenged the serpent's wiles.
He hexed them into jumbie birds,
harbingers of death.

All this occurred on the eighth day,
the Caribbean archipelago a solid gem
before God's furious love shattered it
into a necklace of jades,
strung between North
and South America.

BEHIND THE CARNIVAL

In the beginning was carnival:
the pulse that animated the germ in the soup,
made sperm a triumphant amphibian,
stirred seed to shoot, burned green
in every tree and herb.

The earth became woman's sister
and men hid their awe behind masks,
shaped wood and clay
into images of their fear
behind the carnival.

Behind the carnival
awe turned to dancing rituals;
the moaning was not wind through trees
but gusts of their labours
when lust was innocent
behind the carnival.

Behind the carnival
African gods came out of stones,
gave power to the throb of drum.
Yokes and barracoons could not destroy
deep harmonies of their chanting
behind the carnival.

Behind the carnival
the whipping voice drove slaves
from beds, each one a flambeaux-bearer
coursing with a strength to survive,
dousing cane fields burning up the night
behind the carnival.

Behind the carnival
was a camboulay of dancing torches;
Jabmolasi cavorting, a different fire
in his loins; but that freedom
was as seed-cotton blown in hurricane
behind the carnival.

Behind the carnival
Ma Jake weeps in her chicken pelau,
remembering her daughter who danced
too long in the rain, caught pleurisy
was buried seven days later
behind the carnival.

Behind the carnival
Carmen, saving to play mas,
rakes her mind before coal-pot fire
trying to figure out how to make ends meet
behind the carnival.

Behind the carnival
Boysie argues with his wife,
mother of nine hungry picknies:
He must follow in his father's footsteps
playing midnight robber
even if it's the last thing he does
behind the carnival.

Behind the carnival
no Devil Band for Sharkie this time:
He was practising his wining-up too close
to a woman jamet; he is in hospital now,
balls kicked in
behind the carnival.

Behind the carnival
jumbie owls screech.
They see what no masquerader sees:
the portent in Bad-behaviour sailors' dance,
'Las lap we go beat massa-massa,
las lap we go beat massa-massa.'
behind the carnival.

Behind the carnival
the dragon menaces;
but he is chained by steel
tempered in the hell of sugar plantations
and must learn to dance calypso.
'Hold the dragon,
hold the dragon,'
behind the carnival.

CARNEM LEVARE

They perform a burlesque
of hell's fury: loin fires raging
with roll and thrust of pelvis.

Spectators bordering the way
disguise blushes with sniggerings,
search pockets for coins,
persuade them to dance away:

'Pay de devil, pay
 oh, pay de devil pay!'

Gyrating behind the devils' band
old Father Time, mask precariously awry,
risks revealing his face.

A cloistered Carmelite sister
commits her annual mortal sin
peering through jalousies.
She crosses herself.
Ash Wednesday and another Lent
of chaplets not far away.

FATIGUING THE SOUCOUYANT

With the cocks' first ritual roistering
she puts out her ball of fire.

Back in her creased skin
she is safe from the sun's frizzling.

She suffers endless miles shuffling inches,
until the chalk line on pavement stone
like a barrier of salt to an earthworm;

but her screeching can never break
the foreday morning shuttered gloom,
the nightmares of wrenched roots,
dirge-moans in dark ships holds
where life cuddled death.

Before she can shuffle a turnabout,
little vagabonds materialise:
'Soucouyant Soucouyant, Soucouyant Soucouyant!'

Their chanting is a giddy prance around her.
They do not see tears gathering
with the rheum on her eyes' red rims,
nor the empty skin bags of her breasts quivering.

They will never know the taste
of their blood in her throat.

THE SOUCOUYANT VISITATION

The ball of fire
broke into his night

and on his neck the dry ice
of a kiss
sucking his blood away.

Startled out of sleep,
he shivered in the dark.

From the adjoining room,
a protest of bed springs
and rhythmic moans
heightened the silence.

Next morning,
blue-black blotches
on Lilly's neck
brought back the night.

DOUENS

(Trinidad folklore spirit)

Again those puff-chested
coooo-trills:
Mountain doves in league
with the wind
through willow and bois cano
disguising Douens' cajoleries.

Where Douens' face should be,
a drum-stretched emptiness of skin.
They ventriloquise their chuckling
into air, move with peculiar ease
on feet turned backwards.

Mothers make haste
to christen before death
their sickened babies.
Douens crowd sick cots
or play with shadows
where beaten, bald earth
kept bush at bay.

I wonder who plaits their hair
in such neat rows of cane,
or kisses their smarting bruises?

TERRA-ANIMUS

There is something
in this soil,
where sugar-cane grew
for centuries,
that eyes cannot see,
fingers cannot feel,
nor nostrils smell:

something unspeakable
that made a history
some still suffer with,
others choose
not to write about,

thinking, perhaps,
that words propagate
a life of questions,
a relentless struggle
to find answers.

There is something
in this soil
more than the humus
of dead slaves.

METAMORPHOSIS

Night is a bed of dreams.
I mould the darkness
into images I can touch:
Skin hairs become feathers,
eyes dilate, fill my face;

I am a jumbie bird
in connivance with the night
twisting dreams
into nightmares.

JUMBIE BIRD

In my country
night is a hunting day:
I see where rodents run
and my wings cut the darkness
in a sharp swoop.

Blood has no colour in the night;
only the warm, sticky taste
of flesh ripped.
Death is familiar
as food.

I see the sun
long before it tints the sky.
Then, homing in
to my silk cotton perch
where a fragment of night
is caught in a cluster of leaves,
I close my eyes,
drift into dreams,
slide down a beam of light
to some place where death sits
heavy on the ailing.

Three times I hoot.
Midday catches me sleep-flying,
casting shadows
on a house of grief.

DANCING TO WORDS

for Joan Poulson

On jumbies' happy nights
darkness goes beyond the absence
of moon and stars.
Seeing is with an inner eye.

Owl, jumbie's henchman,
turns night into mischief:
a secret ritual
poets may witness;
a shambling foot-work
to a cacophony of words,
each faux pas a striving
towards making clear,
a new beginning.

THE JON-JON BOYS

Only miracles are expected
beyond this summit on Lavantille's steep:
the pilgrims' atonement-route.

From here sinners' direction is down
through foot-worn paths,
short-cuts through sparse fencing:

a network of links
between ajoupas in this ancient
settlement of soldier slaves

freed from George's war
in North America. They guard
jealously their spunk through

generations; nurture a culture
as earnestly as they husband
their plantains and cush-cush.

When they in the city down-below
light up lamps to flood
spaces the sun abandoned,

the Jon-Jon Boys are still crowned
at their height with setting sun,
beating on pan their rhythms of fight.

STEELBAND DANCING

When dancing
in steelband
dohn hol han.
The way to move
you body,
deserves
serious study.

So lehme give
you some tips,
you mus swing
you hips
this way,
that way,
so an so
like
when you dance
calypso;

and
in road march
when steelband
sweet,
this is the way
to chip you feet.

TRICKSY-LOVE

Even this grey city
is brighter now
as though touched
by your sweet sweet-eye
I ketch fire with.

Strangers smile
when our eyes meet.

Maybe they hear
my calypso heart.
Maybe they are moved
by my dancing walk,

not knowing you,
my Tricksy-Love
who can say so much
without words.

A WISTFUL EUROPEAN SUMMER

Travelling on a French ferry
from Fromentine to L'Ile d'Yeu,
I thought of Caribbean summers,
scudding flying fish, seasoned fishermen
weaving nets and tales for posterity,
salting sea shanties with the heave ho
of their life's rhythm.

I wanted to sing to passengers
of the exploits of Sam Lord, Captain Kidd,
Old Hezikiah who bit a shark on its nose
and lived to tell the tale.

But among les voyageurs crowding decks
there was no mood for such songs.
Their eyes, glazed over with expectation,
gazed at an image of a wanton sun
sizzling skins to bronze.

TRAPPED IN THE ATTIC

They took their sense of sin
to the darkest corner
of the attic where spiders
lived generations of quiet hunting.

In the darkness
touching gave a new life to skin.
Their breathing raised the dust,
entrusted it with secrets.

She made that sound
a bird caught in a fist would make.
'Don't,' she whispered through her shuddering.

The lights went on.
'There is a bird trapped in the attic,'
someone said, climbing the ladder.

MOTHER'S MILK

'You don't understand women,' she says,
turning away from him in bed.

He lies on his side of the rift
remembering mother, grandmother,
great granny on his mother's side,
several aunts, his tomboy cousin May,
all living in cussin distance.

He tells her how when he was a boy
climbing a sapodilla tree with May,
a sapodilla fell in his eye,
how blood flowed buckets.

His grandmother sent him to Neighbour-Beatrice,
who was always having babies.
'One squirt of milk', Grandmother said,
'will do your eye a lot of good.'

Neighbour-Beatrice sat on a stool,
pulled up her dress, trapped him
in the flesh of her thighs.
She unbuttoned her blouse,
released a tumble of breast
just short of suffocation.

A generous squirt in his eye
and milk like a cascade of tears,
soaked him through.

'WELL,' she says, flouncing out of bed,
'that explains A LOT!'

WHAT A WAY TO GO

A sky the colour
of weathered galvanize
was not the burial day
he often joked about
between shots of rum
in the Black Cat Bar.

Coffin-sealed
in his Sunday best,
quiet, first time ever,
he led the way
in a tasselled hearse
relatives closest behind,
then good friends
staccato of heels in the
hushed street.

Women remembered
his dancing hips,
gold-teeth smile,
how he loved a bacchanal.

'Pass de rum, Jacko;
Lehwe fire one fuh Toby.
He woulda like dat.'

That night
wake was good:
whe-whe in the yard,
all-fours
in candle light,
soda biscuits

with steaming coffee
and all the while,
the grief-wailings
disharmonising with
Rock of Ages,
Abide With Me.

He died as he lived;
except that a tom cat
has nine lives.
Toby had only one
too old for sleeping out.
Rumour had it
she was so spent
she couldn't
push him off.

MA JERIMIAH WENT SMILING

Owls hunted no mice
the night Ma Jerimiah's eyes were like
coalpot fire going out.
She was seeing things
invisible to her good neighbours,
disappointed herb healers.

Sister May, the baptist shouter,
gazed through ceiling
to the promised land,
hum-rocking herself into trance.

Ma Jerimiah's voice slipped
between smiling gums.
'Yes Jehova, ah comin, ah comin
in yuh sweet chariot!'

She made to lift herself,
slumped into bedding.
The smile remained.

Owls were heard hooting.
Professional wake goers
crowded the house, knocked back
neat shots of rum,
slapped cards down
in a game of all fours.

From Ma Jerimiah's room
thin hymn-singing voices
silenced the crickets.

BRAVURA

Through jalousies half-closed,
daylight sliced the gloom
with patterned precision,
its cutting edge glinting
on brass knobs
of the four poster bed.

It was time to roll over
in a surf of sheets
and with one foot test
for firm ground;

but leghorn Sam, ignoring
the sun's effort, stretched
his feather-bristling neck,
crowed a rude awakening.

GRANDPA DOLPHUS

When Grandpa Dolphus
pushed car-tyre sandals off,
rubbed apart stuck toes,
you knew he had come in to stay
until next day when rum shop opened.

When he reached for the tin of twist,
trawled pockets for his sweet pipe,
you knew rigmaroles were coming without
the crick-crack-monkey-break-he-back-
on-a-piece-a-pommerac endings.
He swore every single word was gospel.

He told about under silk cotton and sand box trees
where jumbie happenings bristled his hairs
like Grandma's scrubbing brush.
How he made the sign of the cross, ran off
not looking back, not petrifying into salt.
He told how giant forms held the moon
blocked the road, sucked his breath
till he turned about to save his life.

We heard those tales so many times before.
Only the dog gave its dumb attention:
It rolled its eyes in the direction
its listening head should be.

When Grandpa Dolphus pushed Columbus,
our don't-care-a-damn cat, off his lap
you knew his pipe had burnt itself out
like his tales;
but only for that night.

UNCLE CYRIL

Que hay!
A call from across the road.
Shambling towards me, Uncle Cyril,
our family sailor, adventurer
down the Spanish Main, bent
like a question mark
to disguise his six feet four.

Que hay!
El Dorado glinted in his grin.
Hands weathered like good leather
reached out. Carelessness hung about him,
tilted his hat, gave him that look
Grandma called roguish.

His pockets hung heavy with coins.
'Buy sweeties, but don't be lickerish.
Save some fuh yuh brodda an sisters.
How is yuh granma?'

Uncle Cyril had made and lost
a fortune trafficking live stock
to the market in Port-of-Spain,
fishing in his half-owned boat
for anchovies and jacks.

Years later, his seafaring over,
my father found him
consumed by bush lore in a forest
near Charlotteville in Tobago
guarded by a vicious sow,
a butting goat and a parrot screeching:
'Que hay! que hay!'

CRUSOE'S THURSDAY

No room to swing a macajuel
in this survival struggle
of creepers and tall trees.

On the forest floor
wild bananas with their sucker young
stood spotlit from where the high sun
blasted a hole in the roof of green;

he heard Arawak ghosts whispering
as the wind blew
through the bananas' dried leaves,

and when he stopped running,
the forest cleared to a wide grin
of sand, a salty growth of sea almonds
fringing the land end of its lips.

He stood there, face quivering,
shouting to the sea:
'I shall survive this wilderness
with my wit. There is nobody here
but me. That footprint in the sand
is only an illusion.'

But at the first hint of darkness
he was scaling the parapet of tall stakes
at the entrance of his cave.

That night he slept close to the wall
in the farthest corner of his cave
dreaming of tomorrow.

FRIDAY'S SOLILOQUY

There he sits sun-shy
under a parasol of leaves
the sun mottling
his covering of goat skins.

I am used to his strange ways,
no longer fear his flashing arm.
I listen to his stories
about a God beyond the sky,
a devil in a pit of fire.
that never goes out.

I tell him about Bunamuckee,
older than land, sea and sky;
how all things say 'O' to him
and in the end he takes them
into his body. I tell him
about the Oowocakees, the aged ones,
who dare to look at Bunamuckee.
They bring back from the mountains
his wisdoms: sacred images
inscribed on stone.

But I catch the sound 'heathen'
on his breath, hear the panic-flutter
in his voice. He does not know
I see meaning hidden in his words.

Last night in the light of our fire
the salty Caribbean came
to his eyes like full tide.

SCULPTURE EXHIBIT

Catalogued 'Sublime Fruit',
it was more an open mouth
with a tongue shattered
to bits: Gutturals of
a dying griot in Montserrat.

You have to listen hard,
put the bits together.
The tale told
was not of seed pod,
nor the Victorian gloss
of a Caribbean Eden,
but a clay form
hardened off-white,
gravid with ambiguous meanings
in a structured space.

BLOODY BAY TOBAGO

From fisherman's sea view
the nibbled coastline curves:
a beach of white sand,
like a gleaming sickle's edge,
reached by land with tumbling
speed of falling scree.

There is a rankness here
of seamen's tales: Death
by drowning of lovers still
locked together, sperms like spume;
a monstrous carcass eels picked clean
like a ribbed hull caught
in the tide-wash of sand,

This is the place in whose
purple gloom seconds after
the sun's sinking I once heard
the call: 'Baraaacuuudaaaa'.

They return time after time to glut,
memories seared in their brains
of a frenzied feast long ago
when this bay turned red.

OVEN OF CLAY

Your womb: an oven of clay.

In the collective memory of yams:
the health-shine of green leaves,
like hearts of the nation.
In the sun's smile
tender tendrils: umbilical cords
in their halo of fine hairs, nourishing.

Those were better times.

There is tension these days
in the sun's inimitable smile,
stretched over relentless years
of sucking up rivers, lakes,
blood, the tears in yam's eyes.

If only the sun would cease to smile,
pucker the sky's brow with rain clouds.

But still these eternal days of killing light,
and the strain of waiting
for the rumble of crated grain
wheeled through
dust clouds of drought.

CREATIVE SURVIVAL

After the rain storm I am outside
fluttering against glass window.

In its spattered veneer of dust
I scribble verses with my wings:
Voices from the silk cotton tree;
an owl hoots near sick beds at midday.

But I should not try to break glass
with stanzas on old mythologies.
Rain flies lose their wings
with too much fluttering, become
termites again, food for fowl.

MADBULL KITE

Daddie!
Daddie!
Mek a madbull kite
fuh me.
Mek it
big, big, big an ting,
so I could fly it,
not wid coarse tread,
but tick, tick string.
An I go tie it
to a stake
so it cahn escape.
I go mek it
graze up in de clouds
an look down
on dem odder kites
playin at fights;
an people go hear
meh madbull
roarin in de sky
from Lavantie
to Guayaguayare.

JUMBIE TALK

Bet yuh never see a jumbie yet!

Who tell yuh so was foolin yuh.
I see one only lasnite
standin under a silk cotton tree.

Awright, an wey it look like den?

Well, furastart, it kinda tall;
an it like a shadow dat melt in de nite.
It mek a noise like wen yuh blow down
a sweet-drink bottle, yuh know:

woooooooooooooooooooooooommmmmm.

Hey, Rupert!
Rupert, wey yuh dey!
Rupert yuh gone?

RIPITIX, THE ITINERANT COBBLER

Often he came calling,
'Ripitix, Ripitix,'
lips curled the shape of mischief,
shoemaker's knife extended,
keen for cutting.

In my shirt tails
I showed a pair of dusty cheeks,
rhythmic in flight,
my little dangler retracting
like a terrapin.

But that was before
my father's anger
stopped his shameless fooling.

He turned to ambush then,
on my proud way
to nursery school on the block,
past the cedar saw-mill.

It was he who changed
that saw-mill to a monster
with appetite for little boys.
Mill gutters ran blood
the colour of water stained with cedar.

Then one day while the monster screeched,
I could not stop trembling,
made a wish through my tears.

I never saw him again.

SUNDAYS

Sun always shining on Sundays.
Monday-to-Saturday noise gone.

People different on Sundays:
They look so clean.

Daddy gone to market foreday-mornin.
He come back when sun touching house tops,
he come back with watercress
and tie-up blue crab bubbling spit.

Sunday breakfast is cinnamon hot chocolate,
saltfish bull jhol with zaboca and bakes.

Church. And after church,
Sunday school in organdie frocks,
the colour of white sugarcake,
bright colour ribbon in plaits;
navy blue serge pants,
cream silk shirt and panama hat.

Everybody window open wide, wide
showing off frilly lace curtains.
Everybody radio loud, loud
playing the same hymn.

When we come back home
we change in home-clothes.

No marbles on smooth yard ground.
Tops wide awake in pants pocket:
they not sleep-spinning,

humming on the ground.
Sunday sky kite-free.

No brown girl in the ring
with a tra-la-la-la-la;
no hide-and-seek,
no stick-em-up.
Only nancy stories
and Sunday napping.

Sometimes
the man selling icecream
comes just before we fall asleep.
Grandma likes to chat
and we love the icecream.

BREAKING SIESTA

We tip-toed from siesta,
past havens of under-tree shadows,
past our grey clean-neck hen
reddening in midday glare:
Beak open, it was ventilating,
sharp thorn of its tongue stilled;
wing feathers stretched like open fan
in a shallow basin of yard dirt.

We found the cool, dark under-house,
played at secrets: She told me
not to be afraid, it would not bite
if I touched it.
Then, in the fumbling dark
she showed my hand how.

Seconds later I broke free,
saw our leghorn yard cock
treading the grey clean-neck.

BLACK TRIANGLE

It hovered above my head, a black patch
bristling like a dog-scared cat.

Even when a hand came down, scratched it
in the small-window twilight
of the room, it remained silent.

I wanted to reach out and touch it,
but something held me back.

I knew it from somewhere,
that mouth stretched to the limit
and my being forced out
into blinding light, deafening noise
once echoes filtered through water.

I lived again the musk
of closeness, the touch
of a body-warmed chemise,
a nuzzling softness
and sweetness in my throat
to stop me crying.

THE GUARDIAN

No taller than a rose bush,
arms stretched out like a cross,
he spun as though caught
in an eddying wind.

'Stop dilly-dallying, Jason.'
His mother, head full
of saucepans and afternoon tea,
was pretending to leave.

She glanced over her shoulder,
saw him in the daffodils,
heard him chattering,
could not see the elves
dancing around him,
the dark figure
merging with the hawthorn.

NEWS BREAKERS

His was the house scowling
under the stinkin-toe tree,
the flower garden with a rabble
of weeds jostling for air.

They held back, afraid to enter.
How would they tell Ma Chac-Chac?

They felt close to him then,
remembering his school-yard fame
as 'pincher-Jack'. He was snot-taster,
a long range spitter,
expert saliva-bubble-blower.

He was the boy whose mouth watered
peeling dry scabs off healing cuts.

Once he out-ran Mr. Elder's mad dog;
not even the weight of stolen mangoes
stopped his leap to safety.

But this time his leap
was a splintering of bones.
The car never stopped.

YOUNG MAPEPIRE

Survivor of pit nest;
too young to know the dangers
of foot-worn paths near houses,
too innocent to fear Dick,
the polygamous Rhode Island
protecting his harem
from creepy-crawlies,

you slither through a crack
of light into my shut latrine
to feast on anopheles
like stuck darts on the wall,
each abdomen distended blood-black.

You stopped, stared at me, hissed.
My arc through the door was a marvel.

When I picked myself up
I found a killing stone under the aloes,
but the murk had dissolved you.
The mosquitoes were singing.

MANTIS

He nursed
unrequited love
in his green,
heart-shaped
head-of-eyes.

An evolution
of praying for love
has made a crippled
posture of his arms.

Bitterness
has stiffened
his neck,
fanged his limbs
with malice.

In his fierce desires
his embraces kill,
his love devours.

MOSQUITO VIOLINS

Mosquitoes like playing
their violins in the dark;
like the string quartets
Tantie Christine plays
on her moxy gramophone.

When I try to imitate them
in the darkness, they fly
to my mouth, shut me up.

When mosquitoes play music
in the dark I am safe:
they are not sucking blood

CASCADURA REVISITED

We fly higher than cirrus.
From here, miles below are inches.
Time is warped, and not only the jet
trembles through turbulences.

Will my feet still mark mud
where the dasheen used to grow?
Does fermenting hog plum on the ground
still lure ants and butterflies?

Will jamets, tut-tuts loose in frocks,
spit picong words like cherry stones
at wajangs: those molesters on
street corners? (Two of a kind
romanticised in nation language).

Scudding this crop of clouds,
exploded cotton pods in sun,
I hurry into the past,
head full of questions.

THE RETURN

Welcome is tangible hot air
like a cuff in the face.
(Thirty-three years is a long time.)

I too too-toolbay, can't kneel down
to kiss the soil like a good son.

Walking from the plane my footsteps
echo on the tarmac like that time
when I was eager to leave.

I so too-toolbay, I can't think
of searching the Lavantille hills
for that tree nourished as a sapling
on my navel string.

It must be a big tree now,
and like an indulgent mother,
spoiling corn birds, giving its limbs
to their hanging nests.

And where is the old nursery school
on George Street in Port-of-Spain,
shuttered and locked against rioters
back in '38 when Charlie King
was burnt alive in a Southern oil field?

Where it gone, Marine Square with cassia
poinciana and couples strolling.
It's now a bargaining trot along a chain
of ramshackle Rasta boutiques.

But still the smell of energy,
the exuberance of words, colourful
as Assyrians' fabric stores on Charlotte Street,
the urge to spree still burning
unruly as flambeaux in wind;
the calypso heart beat
in the way the body moves.

49

REDISCOVERING LIFE ON WHARTON STREET TRINIDAD

No more that yellow-earth road,
haunt of midnight presences;
but by day, a school boy's practical lesson
in geography: ox-bow lakes,
gorge formations and alluvial deposits.

It is now a pitted asphalt thoroughfare,
signposted Wharton Street, shrunken,
a betrayal of so many fond memories
of my kite-flying, marble-pitching days.

No. 18, my old house, looks smaller
than when I saw it last, back in 1959.
It stands vulnerable,
a forgotten elegance
on tall pillar-trees.

Under its rusted, corrugated iron roof
poverty shows a brave face.
They are the tough ones
from the seeds of forbears,
selected for survival
by the middle passage.

Their priorities instinctive
as coupling: food for the body,
calypso to lift the spirits.

WATCHING THE EYES

Like diving into deep water,
disturbing the settled past.
Thirty-three years abroad

and I have forgotten how
to contrive time
with a will alert for liming.

Here there is a slowing down,
a connivance with circumstance
to prompt a wayward course
of events between spreeing.

And when it comes to getting on
official letters are humbugs;

they diminish opportunities
to blag with more than voice:
the face shifting
from smiles to frowns.

Much more fun
this game of catch the lie
sift reality from fantasy.
Just watch the eyes.

THE REUNION

Four-score years have had
their way with you,
made you like a loose frock
stunning in its time
when you were mother-giver at weddings,
nenen at christenings.

Your sight fails you now,
but you see more clearly
with a mind skilled
at finding its own way
through mangrove terrain.

These days you seldom leave your chair,
replacing argument with a smile,
but I'm glad to see
you kept your sense of humour,
your pampering attentions.

'Oh, never mind me.
Just look after yourself,
live to be a hundred.'

FATHER'S PHOTOGRAPH

After thirty-three years I am back,
goose-fleshed before your photograph.

You stand feet planted square,
straight eye contact; remind me
of that day we stood on the wharf,
words clogged with mutual admirations,
regrets, hopes, things slipping away.

We embraced —we must have.
I boarded the launch which took me
to the *Venezuela* anchored in deep water,
my eyes clinging to you as it sped away.

Half-a-mile out and I could still see
your white hankie in the breeze like a flag.

Now, even in this faded photo,
I see the firm set of your lips
telling so much of your struggle
against all odds. Once when I was twelve
you set me down, explained away
the concept of failure.

I remember the way your shoulders shook
when you laughed; your stubbled chin on my cheek.

You died on a day when I lay cold
in an English town conjuring up pictures
of a Trinidad in fruit-ripening sun.

Yesterday I drove to the burying-ground
in Barataria, was told they had to dig you up
to make room for another.

THE MAN OF THE HOUSE

He had a maco tongue in he mouth
but this time he went too far.
I give-im ah piece ah meh mine.
'If she was here,' I said, 'she wouldn't
want yuh to call she, Tun-Tun'.

He got vex, said how
Caribbean women dohn need
alladat feminist nonsense.
How they strong strong
and in high position in the islands.

That night when he came home
he found a raw breast of chicken.
Pinned to it was a scribbled note:
'Yuh food. Gone to lime with my
sisters in the women's club.'

His cussin set the dogs
in the neighbourhood barking.

CRACK IN THE PEDESTAL

Grave diggers
drenched in the rain,
prepared a place for you.

They were drinking rum
from a broken skull,
protection from
the wandering souls
of bodies they dug up.

Years after that rain
and eyes red with tears,
I come back to a mound of earth
among spring green
where my happy childhood
was buried still
clinging to you.

I stand here wondering who
kept your grave free of weeds.

LANDING ON CRUSOE'S ISLAND

The sea sloped steeply as the plane banked,
began its panoramic sweep down.

Tobago from this height was no larger
than a dark green postage stamp.

Our quick descent telescoped the green,
magnified it to cultivated fields,
trees spattered with blossoms, bright birds.

In a field embroidered with furrows
a scarlet ibis flaunted its landing skill.

We landed with a bump, sped sea-ward
down a runway, veered at the last minute,
taxied to our designated parking.

We came off the plane into glaring heat
like into some unfamiliar element.
Instinct was to run, seek out a cool place.

'Home, this is home,' squawked a corn bird
above the boom and wash of the sea
always never far away.

LA CUISINE DE LAUTREC

I

Henri knows from their hunting
recipes together that Maurice
would kill for a plate of pistou.

It is easy enough boiling
vegetables into anonymity.
Now there is a fretting in the
marmite like a mud volcano.
Henri knows that the pistou paste
is what redeems this potage.

With mortar and pestle
he persuades into polygamy
garlic and basil, tomatoes
steamed, peeled and seeded;

but there is trauma
in this ménage à trois,
till gruyère and olive oil
are introduced, and PISTOU!
The paste is made. Henri
stirs it in with a wooden spoon.
(Tasting for adjustments
is superfluous, a mere habit.)

Smiling, he moves to open
the front door. Half way there,
the door bell rings. Maurice
waits to be let in.

II

After bottles of port spiced
with nutmeg, a brisk swim
in the Seine to clear his head;
then to Le Chat Noir
to delight in musk interiors,
crayons merciless as his wit.

Mimi came up, smothered him
with softness, distorted
his pince-nez, made him think
of mother. Another bottle
of port and maybe he could
entice her to his atelier with
promises of last night's pistou.

DRAWING AT 24 RUE DES MOULINS

His final flourish
of chalk pastel
to his drawing of Mimi
between customers,
was like a garni of
parsley to his dish
of roast lamb.

'Voilà,' he would say,
'un très bon gigot.'

She would slip
into silk cami-knickers,
look at his drawing.

'Petit méchant,'
she would say, kissing him
on the forehead
and tugging gently
at his beard.

FEAR OF FALLING

'There's no danger, Henri,
doing it like this.
Falling off that horse
was a long, long time ago.

Stand on this stool.
Steady yourself holding
on to my shoulders.

And Henri,
this one is on me,
take your time about it.

Just think of your
'Pied de Mouton à la Poulette
gently simmering
for four hours.'

Eyes shut tight,
Henri felt things
closing in on him.
His cry of 'Maman'
came muffled.

POULET MORENGO

In preparing this dish
what he enjoys most
is making that tame bird
as wild as a coq de bruyère.

He sets it free
from the fowl-run, pursues it
into open country, shoots it
with fine buck shot.

'There must be other ways,
just as quick,
to make a chicken tender,'
his mother often tells him;
(and this from an aristocratic
hunting family).

Nevertheless,
she eats heartily his Poulet Morengo,
praises its succulence.

THE OTHER SIDE OF LAUTREC

I

I wonder if Henri takes his onions
to keep la grippe away.
Always been delicate, that boy.

I blame Alphonse. The Toulouses
have a poor constitution;
and horny as wild rabbits.
I must admit though,
I sleep earlier at nights
now that his father is maudlin,
takes to his chaise-longue.

Poor Henri! He never did recover
falling off that horse. He has kept
close to the ground ever since.

II

Henri may as well be naked
lying across the bed in his Paris flat,
his night shirt crumpled short
by restless sleep.

Last night's Soup à l'Oignon
lingers like a lover not wanting to leave.

His nostrils quiver. He stirs, licks his lips.
Opening his eyes he sees pink knickers
hanging on les cadavres of wine bottles.

'Colette must have been in a hurry.'
He smiles as he runs his fingers
over the drawings in his sketch pad.

III

Henri cooks for his friends tonight:
Joyant, Vuillard, Paul Leclercq and
George Henri-Manuel, the fastidious one.

Everything must be au point:
Lobster à l'Américaine, followed, not too close
by roast veal, giving time to bavarder,
help the digestion.

To punctuate this passage of savouries,
endives rolled in thin slices of ham
with a cheese sauce as intimate companion;

and after a suitable period of discussion,
perhaps on the lethal charms of Jane Avril
currently dancing at the Moulin Rouge,
the Reblochon with a chilled Chablis.

For dessert, la pièce de résistance:
His new Degas in the salon.

THE RIVALS

In desperation to exist,
she stuck her lips
to the feet of Descartes.

She ignored suitors, remained indoors,
afraid, even when blossoms fell
like confetti and people went dancing
around maypoles.

She was afraid to come out
when birds were doing what bees also do
and lascivious boars followed false trails
rutting found truffles.

She ignored the suitors beneath her window
singing like black birds in Spring.

When they grew tired,
they put their libido through
something resembling abuse,
resorted to thinking,
that all things considered,
Freud had got it wrong.

SHOOTING STARS OVER FARMERS' FIELDS

That summer I wish you were with me
tasting the succulence of that road-side peach
as sweet as any pommerac.

And if that summer you were with me
to gaze at stars shooting
over farmers' fields in Normandy,
how your breasts would have heaved
on a wishing sigh, those stars
no match for your eyes.

I wish you here now far from that summer
observing how this chilled spring breeze
worries the cherry blossoms
in a garden across the street;

then we could sit believing
there is a sun somewhere above
this slapdash wash of grey
and hear black bird with its wistful song.

AT THE GREEN GROCER'S

He blushed
at the tomatoes'
plumpness;
preferred the ones
that gave a little
when squeezed;

felt an odd sense
of pride seeing
the firm cucumbers
in plastic skins.

He stopped short,
relaxing forefinger
and thumb, inches
from the pert
raspberries.

Embarrassed,
he looked away,
observed a woman
peel a banana,
bite into it.

PAPA BOIS

I was the child frightened
by your old man's puckish grin:
raw gash across your forest face
like a dry season ravine.

I heard moonlight tales about you:
how you took with magic ease the deer's form,
turned hunters into the animals they hunted.

You wrote the bush lore book
on leaves of trees and blades of grass.

With your breath you scribbled
on the surface of evaporating pools
counsel for easy fishing to the water fowl.

You were voyeur and conniver
in La Jabless's fatal coquetry,
laying snares like Venus man-traps
for romantic saga-boys who seek her favours.

Oh spare me your noose of vines.
I am no agouti chaser, no laglee setter.
My venture into your forest, twilight world
was the lure of your bush wisdom.

John Lyons was born in Trinidad and educated at Goldsmith's College. He lives in Manchester. He has been twice winner of the Peterloo Poets Afro-Caribbean/Asian prize, and has been in many anthologies. As a painter he has exhibited both nationally and internationally. He has also been the selector of national touring exhibitions and a purchaser for the Arts Council national collection.

Smith/Doorstop Books

publish books, cassettes
and pamphlets by

Moniza Alvi	Geoff Hattersley
Simon Armitage	Jeanette Hattersley
Sujata Bhatt	Keith Jafrate
Liz Cashdan	Mimi Khalvati
Julia Casterton	John Lancaster
Linda Chase	Peter Lane
Debjani Chatterjee	John Lyons
Bob Cooper	Ian McMillan
Tim Cumming	Cheryl Martin
Duncan Curry	Paul Matthews
Peter Daniels	Eleanor Maxted
Joyce Darke	David Morley
Owen Davis	Les Murray
Carol Ann Duffy	Pascale Petit
Anna Fissler	Lemn Sissay
Sophie Hannah	Joan Jobe Smith
John Harvey	Mary Woodward
Jo Haslam	Cliff Yates